T0210050

POEMS TO SHOW YOU'RE NOT ALONE

BRINGING LIGHT TO THE DARKNESS
OF MENTAL HEALTH

KATARINA ELISABETH

authorHOUSE®

AuthorHouse™
1663 Liberty Drive
Bloomington, IN 47403
www.authorhouse.com
Phone: 1 (800) 839-8640

Published by AuthorHouse 02/25/2019

ISBN: 978-1-5462-7998-3 (sc)
ISBN: 978-1-5462-7997-6 (e)

Print information available on the last page.

Any people depicted in stock imagery provided by Getty Images are models, and such images are being used for illustrative purposes only.
Certain stock imagery © Getty Images.

This book is printed on acid-free paper.

Because of the dynamic nature of the Internet, any web addresses or links contained in this book may have changed since publication and may no longer be valid. The views expressed in this work are solely those of the author and do not necessarily reflect the views of the publisher, and the publisher hereby disclaims any responsibility for them.

Dedicated to Laurie, Olivia, Julia, Kylie, Lorin,
Ms. Ganuelas, and my family

You will never leave my heart

CONTENTS

EXPRESSIONS OF DARKNESS

EXPRESSIONS OF LIGHT

PART 1

EXPRESSIONS OF DARKNESS

ESCAPE

I write all these poems to quiet my need
To self-harm, swim in shame, and the thoughts that just feed
On the idea that I'll never have happiness or joy.
These thoughts that think they're so sneaky and coy.
But they're pain and destruction inside of my mind
And I write all these poems so that I can find
Some release and some freedom not fame and applause.
These poems help me escape and they fight the true cause:
They bring light to the darkness as I shout to the void.
I know this pain's constant and I still get annoyed
That it won't go away, and I'll never be healed
But that doesn't mean that I must stay concealed.
And once I have learned how to handle the strife
I'll be able to go make the most of my life.

Panic

I'm walking and working
And all is fine.
Then, everything feels wrong
Without a sign.

My chest feels so tight
I can barely breathe.
I cry, and I gasp,
As my insides seethe.

I'm shaking and dizzy
And I can't feel my hands.
Why must I feel like this?
I don't understand.

My throat starts to tighten
As my legs start to wobble.
I try to appear normal
As my thoughts start to squabble.

Can someone please tell me,
How long will this last?
What do I do
When an hour has passed?

After the attack
Is finally done,
It takes over a day
Until the effects are gone.

MISWIRED

Anxiety controls me
When I'm feeling too much.
Depression weighs me down,
It feels like a crutch.

Some people don't realize
That there's something else;
An emotion that creates
An empty self.

Instead of emotions,
I only feel blank.
No happy, no sad.
Should I give thanks?

Complete apathy
About every decision.
No feelings, no thoughts,
No desires or visions.

Sometimes, this vacancy
Lasts for a second.
Sometimes, it's much longer
Than what is expected.

How weird it feels
To feel nothing at all.
Maybe I'm just experiencing
A faulty protocol.

Faux

Masks are well developed
In the world which we reside.
For we see only smiles
When, inside, the person's died.

We choose to judge each other
On which mask we like the best.
We throw away the real ones
Because we like the fake ones best.

I wonder, what would happen
If the world became a place
Where no one chose to hide behind
A sick, distorted face.

GLITCH

My brain is working normally
When, abruptly, I feel shocked.
I try to regain access
But my brain is adeptly locked.

I turn on autopilot
To figure out what to do
To appear as if nothing has happened,
To hide it all from you.

My processes aren't working
And I don't know what it means.
It's like everyone else is playing
While I'm stuck on a loading screen.

I notice it's not working
When I see you start to frown.
Sorry, I can't help it:
My system's shutting down.

As I'm starting to grow numb,
I can feel my fingers twitch.
I wonder when you'll figure out
That I am just a glitch.

SILENCED

Pay attention to voices
For they are a powerful thing.
One can yell or whisper
While another screams or sings.

Every chosen word
And every minute inflection
Can give the listener data
About the speaker's inner reflection.

Words of joy
Turn to words of hate.
Every word
Can decide someone's fate.

Something spoken in hate
Can end someone's existence
For it might strengthen a
Harmful thought's persistence.

Words can manipulate
And scare and abuse.
Each word has power,
So be careful to choose.

Statements that someone
May say in passing
Can have an effect
That is everlasting.

People tell themselves
That they don't have a choice
As they continue to spew words
That end someone else's voice.

This world is already
Full of violence
And full of voices
That have already been silenced.

Knives and guns
May break my skin
But words do irreparable
Damage within.

INVISIBLE

Everybody knows me,
I'm the one you never see.
Everyone ignores me
Like an unspoken decree.

My features aren't special,
So, I'm easy to overlook.
No one even notices
When I hide behind a book.

I'm the one that startles you
When you realize I'm there.
You know that I exist,
You just don't really care.

I feel like a one-way mirror
Because I can see right through,
Though, when you try to see me
I just choose to reflect you.

It's a safety mechanism
Since I've spent my whole life hiding.
I'm perplexed trying to join
What I have spent my life dividing.

Maybe I just inherited
An isolation gene.
I'm terrified of knowing
That one day I might be seen.

ALONE

I know all the monsters from under my bed.
They all tried to get me and wished I was dead.
But, as I got older and faced all my fears,
I'm still overwhelmed, and I can't hide my tears
Because now I know something that fills me with dread:
The worst are the monsters inside of my head.

I struggle to cope with a mind that swears
That everyone leaves, and nobody cares.
Because no matter what the idea just won't stick.
My brain is so broken I think love's a trick.
No matter how much I need someone to love me,
It's not worth the heartbreak so just let me be.

UNREALISTIC

No matter how much you listen
Or how much you preach,
The life that you want always seems
Just out of reach.

In a world full of mourning and illness,
With so many poor,
We hear all the stories
And chose to ignore.

We shrug in indifference
When we see the news
Because we have accepted
That we'll always lose.

In this world full of murder
And betrayal and lies,
We continue to do nothing
As innocents die.

We send kids to school
But inside we say,
"Will my child live
To the end of the day?

The people wear masks
As they hide all their scars.
"Maybe we'll find true relief
In one of these bars."

The world looks around
Like the answer's elusive
As it covers the truth
Of a past that's abusive.

This is brought up
With grace and with tact:
The world won't change
If you don't choose to act.

We could live in a helpful world
Where no one is homeless or sick.
Instead, we throw away food while others starve.
Which one should be unrealistic?

People do anything
To find some relief
When we should be encouraging
Self-love and belief.

Alcohol and drugs
For those trying to numb
All the chaos of which
Addiction's just a symptom

Try to start
With a simple choice:
Don't let anyone
Silence your voice.

CONFUSION

I don't look in the mirror
Because I don't really get.
How can someone look and me
And see someone to spend time with?

Don't they know I'm stupid
And I wish that I was dead?
I constantly fight myself,
I've cut until I've bled.

Do they think that they can save me
From the darkness that's inside?
Would they choose to love me
If they knew I'd chosen to die?

I'm struggling to survive amidst
The chaos from my youth.
Would you choose to be around me
If I always spoke my truth?

I know there's days I'm great
And I can always make you smile.
But when the sun has gone away
Would you also disappear for a while?

Katarina Elisabeth

I guess I'm just confused about
What I should pretend to be.
I want someone to love me for being
Completely, authentically, me.

GULLIBLE

You told me that you love me
But, right now, I'm just confused.
For beneath all the love and joy
I was left just feeling used.

Yet still I wish with every morn
That you will pass my way.
How foolish I must have been
To think that you would stay.

I guess that I should thank you
Because I've accepted this milestone:
No matter what someone says
I'll perpetually end up alone.

ADDICT

I thought as the time went by,
The urge would go away.
This need inside still haunts me
Almost every single day.

How is it possible for anyone
To live and feel like this?
Toxic needs that eat away inside
And even when fed don't dismiss.

As soon as you falter,
The need just increases.
You feed more and more
But it never ceases.

When I am in
My happiest moment,
The need overwhelms me
Without my consent.

How am I supposed to be honest and say
That I am not doing well?
How can I look inside their eyes
And say I feel trapped in Hell?

SELF-HARM

How badly I want all my urges to ease.
I'm tired of fighting this mental disease.
Though I know that this knife
May one day take my life
My emotions still beg for release.

The world only wants people who know how to thrive.
It only wants people who want to be alive.
It wants the people labeled as superb.
It doesn't want me because I am disturbed
And I'm tired of trying to survive.

As more scars form along my skin,
The pain doesn't match what I feel within.
I know that there's a fatal risk.
My actions are calculated and brisk.
Still, I wish for a new life to begin.

HIDE

I see you react to the scars on my skin
I cringe as all the judgement begins
I thought I could trust you
But I guess that's not true
So, I'll hide all the scars from within

Because with your eyes you think you have spied
Something that proves that inside I have died
But what you don't see
Cause you didn't see the real me
Is that they show all the times I've survived

ABUSE

You see my stress
And assume impatience.
You see I have problems
With human relations.

You assume my intelligence
Based on emotions
But behind how I feel
Is passion and devotion.

I'm working. I'm trying.
Don't judge at first glance.
I can excel if you
Just give me a chance.

DARKNESS

I honestly don't know why I started writing
Because in my head I would rather be dying.
All I want for myself now is pain.
I guess part of me still hopes for some rain,
To feel little droplets of water come down.
Is it too much to ask that I drown?
Please, someone, please put a gun to my head;
People seem better when it's a homicide instead
Of being that person that offs themselves.
I wish I could store all these thoughts on a shelf.
I feel like a prisoner inside of my body
Especially with a mind that is fighting to kill me.
I'm sorry if this makes you panicked or scared.
I would rather just help you to be prepared
To fight with both thoughts and reality.
To know that each day might somehow be
The one where you stop and take your last breath.
Everyone at some point must face their death.

HOPELESS

I know that I need to escape from this darkness.
I've tried for so long that I just feel so hopeless.
The thoughts in my head
That I'm better off dead
And I struggle to sleep
Cause the nightmares run deep
I'm still trapped when I wake
Cause the darkness just takes
The small glimmer of hope
At the end of this rope
And tells me I'll fail
As I feel my soul wail
I just want to be free
Of this terror in me
Cause the meds just don't work
And the darkness just smirks
Cause it knows I can't leave
I'm stuck trying to grieve
The life I could've had
Where I could've been glad
But I'm stuck in this world
With the darkness unfurled
And I no longer know how to be

HOLE

I'm tired of feeling so much emotion.
It's like every decision is a life or death situation.
If I mess up or make a mistake
I think of every way I can take
My life. I know it sounds dumb
But I'm tired of feeling everything yet at the same time feel numb.
Even the good ones like joy and love
I am getting so sick and tired of
Because once I feel them, I feel them so deeply
That when they are gone there is a hole in me.

HEARTBREAK

Everyone thinks the heartbreak that is worst
Is the one that is your very first,
What about all the times when
Your heart breaks again and again?
That time when they again break your trust?
Or when someone you love did something unjust?
But I know now the one that hurts worst of all
Is the one where you just completely fall
In love with a person after you'd already given up.
The one where you'd already emptied your cup.
They break down your wall and step inside
And they saved you when you should have died.
When you finally believe there's one person who'll never leave you,
You blink and then they do.

ABANDONED

I honestly don't know if I have any more tears.
I feel like someone has confirmed all my fears That
no one truly loves me and thinks that I'm worth The
pain and the heartache. I regret my birth.
Right now, I'm so broken and now I feel dry.
I want to be dead, but I can't even try
Because I don't want to accept what happens if I fail:
I'll no longer be able to hide behind the masquerade fairytale.
I want to self-harm. All that I know is hurt.
It's like someone saw my pain and then rubbed it in dirt.
For some reason, I'm still here but I feel like I've been dropped
Off a cliff because it feels like my heart has stopped.

SUNSET

I didn't want a future but then I found one
Where I could be happy and want to have fun.
But now all that I want to do is run.
I've tried so many times and right now I'm just done.
It's like every time that I think that I've won,
I'm thrown something worse before I've begun.
I'm looking for hope and right now I see none.
In my head all that I see is a gun,
So, I think that this time I will set with the sun.

BLACKOUT

I found a new light and in a second it was gone.
I try to find more but the curtains are drawn.
What's the point of finding more light
When it doesn't stay for long in this never-ending night?
My mind is caught in dark hyperbole
Nothing makes sense and I just want to flee.
I'm tired of living this life monotone
And I'm weary of waiting for the hateful unknown.
I just want to leave myself behind.
I am tired of the constant fight with my mind.

SLEEPING

How can I begin to explain
That I am afraid of sleeping?
I fight against exhaustion
While inside I am weeping.

I try to stay up
For as long as I can
But so far that is never
A very good plan.

How can I explain
Why my work's not effective?
"Oh, sorry! I just have
A brain that's defective.

I see people die in dreams
And I watch while they suffer.
My dream makes me
Brush my teeth with a razor.

Or the dreams with the centipedes,
Spiders, and cockroaches
Inside every crevice?
Or when a demon approaches?

I'm burned, and I'm stabbed,
And I'm shot, and I'm killed.
There are the psychological ones
Where I actually build

A family, fall in love,
And live a whole life.
I'm somebody's mom
And I'm somebody's wife.

And when I'm completely convinced
That someone fully loves me and needs me,
I wake up and remember things
That no one should ever see."

And, though it is true
All the stuff that I wrote,
I don't think they will give me
A doctor's note.

TIRED

I'm tired of being afraid of the night:
Of sleeping and darkness, nightmares filled with fright.
How badly I want all this terror to cease.
Nightmares are even my earliest memories.
I'm stuck with the fact that they won't go away.
I know so many people but I'm the one that must pay
The price of a good night's sleep.
I try to forget but my mind makes me keep
All the darkness and terror and murder and pain.
I'm sorry but seriously what do I gain
By having a brain so twisted and broken?
I hide all the nightmares and I've barely spoken
About all the worst ones or ones that confuse,
Ones that make me relive so much mental abuse
Where I can't even tell if I'm asleep or awake.
I don't know how much more of this I can take.
I'm trying to process and see how I feel
But I'm scared because I no longer know what is real.

AWAKE

I struggle to think as I try to decide
Am I awake? Or am I trapped inside
Of my brain that enjoys when I'm tortured relentlessly
With nightmares filled with horrors that no one should ever see
The characters worry and crease their brows
As they tell me that I am in the here and now.
But something feels fuzzy like I am still dreaming
And inside my confusion is quietly screaming.
I specifically try to look for the details
To prove I am dreaming but everything fails.
I'm feeling desperate as I creep to the ledge.
The answer is found at this building's edge.
So now here's my question: Am I asleep?
Will I awake after taking this leap?

BROKEN

When I was young, I would imagine
All kinds of worlds that I'd want to live in;
Worlds full of stories of magic and adventure,
Places where I could be sure
That I wanted to wake up tomorrow.
Instead, I live in a world of sorrow.
A world full of terror and death and disease.
I go for the flowers and get stung by the bees.
My body will hurt, and I'll always be sick:
Pain, inflammation, and asthma are classified as chronic.
"At least," I think, "I still have my brain."
I try to hold on but the thoughts they just drain
All my energy. I can't get out of bed
Cause my mind constantly tells me that I'm better off dead.
Then, after years of falling apart,
I finally see that I still have my heart.
But quicker than that thought can be spoken,
I take a step and it's already broken.

Choice

Puzzle pieces are beautiful
When they all find their match.
Amidst all the chaos
They have somewhere to attach.

Some pieces travel throughout their life
And never seem to fit.
Puzzle after puzzle,
They search and refuse to quit.

Days turn into weeks
As the weeks turn into decades.
Every lonely second,
Others watch as their hope fades.

Every time they thought they found
A puzzle where they belong,
The other pieces shove them out
And tell them they are wrong.

Now the piece must make a choice,
Should it keep on trying?
Or should it stop and realize
That they are better off dying?

TWISTED

My brain was filled with poison
As my somber thoughts persisted.
I hoped that they would disappear
But they became more twisted.

I began to dream about
When Death and I would meet.
I no longer cared to look
Before I crossed the street.

I glanced at every building
And I studied every bridge
To see which ones were tall enough
Should I step off the ledge.

I contemplated weapons
And I studied the statistics.
To see what's most effective,
I looked at the logistics.

Every time I traveled
I would say a little prayer
For a quick and painless accident
With no one else impaired.

I no longer want to die
But I still feel conflicted.
I have had these thoughts so long
I think I am addicted.

DEREALIZATION

Everything gets fuzzy
And I can't tell what's real.
It's like the world is spinning
And I can't tell how I feel.

My mind starts to wander
And I visualize other places
Where the world is full of peace and love
With smiles on people's faces.

But everyone here looks at me
And I feel like I am drugged.
As if the world's a simulation
And, somehow, I have been unplugged.

It's like I'm trapped inside a dream
And I cannot awake
But this world feels like a nightmare;
So, I pray that it is fake.

PART 2

EXPRESSIONS OF LIGHT

PAUSE

Today, I'm feeling sorrow as I look back at my past.
I mourn the things I could've had and things that didn't last.
I need some time to process now so I can start to grow.
I have the choice to stop fueling this tumultuous tornado.
We have the choice to be ourselves and find out how to stop concealing.
Maybe we'll one day find the way to some discordant healing.

HOPE

I think I'm eternally trapped in this maze.
I wish I could think but I'm in such a daze
That I can't remember if I've gone left or right.
It's dark because I'm stuck in a never-ending night
Where the stars are too dim and there isn't a moon.
I feel like I'm imprisoned in a broken cocoon.
I wish more than anything that I could get out.
I hope for escape as I scream and I shout.
But something else happens as I go along:
I become more alive and I'm filled with a song.
I made one more turn and I found a dead end.
I didn't expect that I would find a friend.
There's someone who understands all the confusion.
Someone else who is trapped with the constant intrusion
Of thoughts that all say "To be free is to die.
You'll be stuck in this maze and there's no reason why.
You'll be trapped and afraid and alone in the dark."
But now I'm not alone so I know there's a stark
Difference between the truth and my thoughts.
I look back at the times when I cried and I fought.
Now, I know there is someone beside me on my journey
Even though we both know we may never be free.
And though sometimes it feels like we're trapped in a tomb,
It only takes one light to brighten a dark room.

TEARS

My emotions don't know
How to be expressed.
They all pile up
And I'm always depressed.

They build up inside
As I keep them all hidden.
My brain thinks vulnerability
Is something forbidden.

I aptly overlook
As they pile up tall.
I guess I have just
Gotten used to the wall.

Some days I reach
My emotional limit.
I shove them all in
But they no longer fit.

The thought of being open
Is one of my biggest fears.
Eventually, I can no longer hide
As my pain overflows into tears.

The weight is slowly lifted
And my brain struggles with disbelief.
I thought crying would make it heavier
But instead I find relief.

STRENGTH

Life feels so dark like everything is wrong.
The world pushes forward while you're dragged along.
It's like you're the princess who's stolen and trapped
Who will never be free and is forced to adapt
To the world you don't deserve and never should've had
Where you try to find good and you're swallowed in bad.
But then after years of being stuck in the tower
You realize the truth that makes everyone cower.
The reason you're locked up is not what you thought.
If you'd known the truth all those times that you'd fought
You would see you're not trapped or weak or unwanted;
The darkness wants to keep you where you're stuck feeling daunted.
You're not weak, ugly, crazy, or any similar things:
You are the dragon with fire and wings.
The reason the darkness is sticking like glue
Is because once you see your strength, there's no stopping you.

MAGIC

You've been told there's no magic on Earth.
This lie's been ingrained in your head since birth.
Though you can't see it with your eyes,
That is not where magic lies.
Whether you're in the darkest dark or the brightest light,
The happiest day or the hardest night,
I have a secret that I will impart:
True magic is found within your mind and heart.
Though all the emotions you can't really see,
The heart inspires creativity.
Just close your eyes and slowly inhale
And imagine along as I share this tale:
After spending all night tossing and turning
You awake to the smell of something burning.
You jump up in a panic and run to see
That as you get closer, it changes to coffee.
As you reach the kitchen, another smell comes
Of bacon and eggs and cinnamon buns.
You close your eyes to enjoy these fresh smells
And when your eyes open you see people you know well.
Loved ones smile and laugh and give you a kiss.
You're overwhelmed by the feelings of bliss.
After you're done, you glance out the window
And see that everything is covered in snow.

You open the door and feel the sharp cold
And you think of the holiday stories you've been told.
You step outside while your loved one bakes
And tilt your head back to catch some snowflakes.
Just for a second, you feel only joy
As you watch a snow fight between girls and boys.
You walk back inside and the cold starts to melt.
You get some hot chocolate and cautiously knelt
In front of the fire with your favorite book.
You fit perfectly in a comfortable nook.
Breathe in the smells and feel yourself smile;
Let yourself live in this time for a while.
Now, wiggle your fingers and wiggle your nose
And imagine the smell of a rose.
Even though you haven't been anywhere,
It truly feels like you really were there.
If that isn't magic, then I don't know what is.
I don't think that we can dismiss
Our feelings and thoughts and our passion inside
Of us is where the true magic lies.

AWKWARD

I've spent my life hiding behind
A perfectionistic scam.
I've tried so long to fit in
That I don't know who I am.

People seem to judge me
When I feel stressed and confused.
Would they give me patience
If they know I was abused?

I want to be true to myself
And be authentically me.
I've spent my life just playing parts.
Who am I supposed to be?

Now I finally realize,
No matter how many times I have tried,
I don't have to give up.
I can start over and decide.

HOME

The world became unmanageable
As everyone faced pain and loss.
Society imploded as
It all spiraled into chaos.

Those who rose above it all
Were those who had learned how to cope.
They had already learned to face the dark
And still cling onto hope.

For we are so much stronger
Than our brains would have us believe.
Our brains tell us we are worthless burdens
But we are being deceived.

We learned to ride the waves of stress
And battle our inner demons.
We're at home amongst the chaos
Because we've lived there through every season.

CANDLE

You are a simple candle
With a single glowing flame.
If you think that you are meaningless,
Then society is to blame.

For though you may be small right now,
You contain so much power.
You can grow so brilliant that you
Shine even in April showers.

Not only can you grow and shine,
You can choose to give.
By helping others light the dark,
You can help them choose to live.

ONE

I thought that I never
Deserved to be heard
And that my thoughts
Would forever be blurred

Despite the love,
I felt the hate
And assumed that pain
Was my only fate.

I dealt with my issues
The best I knew how.
That doesn't mean
It's the best way now.

The people who love me
Until I love myself
Encourage me and show me that
The world can be something else.

Now I don't write for the masses,
To make myself whole;
I write for the hope
That I can lighten one soul.

TRUTH

I'm ugly. I'm fat.
I'm alone and I'm broken.
To me, truer words
Have never been spoken.

I believe I'm alone
With the thoughts in my head
That panic and assume
My best self is being dead.

You see the pain in my eyes
And, on my arms, all the lines.
It's enough that you don't believe me
When I say that I'm fine.

To you, I am labeled as
Perfectly imperfect.
You think I'm worth love
And deserve to connect.

You've never even met me
But your heart says it's true.
If it's true about me
I know it's true about you.

WAITING

I've spent so long
Inside of Hell
Until I realized that
I have a story to tell

Of darkness and terror
And finding some light.
I want to help others
As they fight the same fight.

I want to show others
That they're not alone.
The lesson I learned
Is just trying to postpone.

The plan, the rehearsal,
The moment you act.
You're important and unique
And that is a fact.

Please, give yourself mercy;
Tomorrow's a new day.
If someone else had these thoughts
Then what would you say?

The hardest thing is
That the choice is only yours.
I wish I could give something
That would erase the dark core.

I wish I could promise
A lifetime of good health
Where nothing goes wrong and
You're blessed with love and wealth.

All I can tell you is that
I understand.
Stuck in my shame,
My death was all planned.

I thought that I
Was alone with my thoughts.
I cried and I broke
And I constantly fought.

But if you choose this now
You will miss when life brings
The moments that make it
Worth the waiting.

PEACE

Relax your shoulders,
Calm your mind.
Do what you need
To breathe and unwind.

Imagine the snow
As it lands in your hair
And quiets the world,
So graceful and fair.

The waves of the ocean
That hold you and sway
And the peace as it carries
Your anguish away.

The moment you pause
As the music reaches in
To rekindle and embolden
Your strength found within.

The wind as it whispers
The secrets unfurled
And carries your wishes
To voyage the world.

When you watch as the darkness
And maledictions increase,
Don't let your heart forget
The moments of peace.

MOMENTS

For some reason, I'm having a small inclination
To write a poem for some inspiration.
I can't handle this overwhelming emotion
So, I imagine the waves of the ocean
That slowly come and go away.
How about the sun at the end of the day
With an explosion of purple, red, blue, and yellow?
Or the moment you first told your crush "hello"?
Sitting around while speaking of lore
As you inhale them smell of a smore.
The coal is red and the fire crackles
And just for a moment you're free of the shackles
That constantly control your body and mind.
Let's see what other moments we can find.
How about the idea of your very first kiss?
If I kill myself now, I will forever miss
All the moments where life proves me wrong.
How about writing your very own song
With words that fully express what you mean?
How about that feeling when everything is clean?
If I decide now this is all that I get,
What about all the animals I'll never get to pet?
Or all the music that I'll never get to hear?
I'll never get to memorize Shakespeare.

All the candles I'll never get to light?
Or all the music that I'll never get to write?
All the plays that I'll never get to see
Because I decided I no longer want to be me.
All the flavors I'll never get to taste
And that time spent in school will have just been a waste.
I'd never find love
And I'd never get married.
I'd never experience the first time that I carried
A baby that came from the womb of a friend
Because I chose right now that I want to end
My life and give up these times.
I'd never again hear wind chimes.
I know that right now I feel like I'm suffering
But sometimes the things that keep me from dying
Aren't always big like engagement bling.
Sometimes, it's small like an oven ding.
The smell of your favorite treat
May be all that you need to not admit defeat.

SPRING

She watches as the branches
Dance gracefully in the breeze.
She looks around at the beautiful world
That no one else pauses to see.

She stops for the flowers
While others race by.
There are so many people
Yet not one says "hi".

She notices smiles and
Worry and frowns.
She tries to look up
While others look down.

She notices leaves and the
Clouds in the sky,
The exhausted and
The twinkling eyes.

The scurrying animals
Racing along,
She tries to hear
As the world sings its song.

Katarina Elisabeth

The butterfly passes
And flutters its wings
As the earth releases
The hope that spring brings.

The world that,
Only a few months ago,
Was colorless and freezing
While covered and snow.

For the time being her mind fights
Against dark and cold
But she clings to the idea
That soon hope will unfold.

Sun

The sun reminds us
Of our worth.
It brings new life
And provides rebirth.

The days that follow
The hardest nights,
The sun still shines
Its brightest light.

It reminds us that we
Can start again.
There's been light in the darkness
Since time began.

At night, it tells us
It's ok to rest;
Having proper self-care
Makes us our best.

Don't let anyone tell you
What you do and don't deserve.
Don't forget that your voice
Deserves to be heard.

Essence

The smallest light inside of you
Can light the darkest place.
You have no more reason to hide
As the tears stream down you face.

I don't need to remind you
That time is of the essence.
But allow me to express the idea
Of bioluminescence.

Instead of producing light from things
Like gas and electricity,
It proves that there can be a light
The can from you and me.

And though we still face harder days
And endless chaotic nights,
Time is of the essence.
So, don't give up your fight

CONTROL

From this moment on,
Something's changed for me.
I've decided to become
The best that I can be.

I'll try to love those who hate
And I'll help those in pain.
I'll choose to do good
When there's nothing to gain.

Though there may be times
When I still feel trapped,
It is my choice now
To learn to adapt.

I'm the only thing
That I can control.
I want to help others
Achieve dreams and goals.

God, please give me wisdom
And the heart to see
That I can't change the world
But I can change me.

EXTINGUISHED

I once felt within me
A burning desire.
I was strong and passionate
And full of fire.

I helped provide light
And helped others stay warm.
I tried to provide hope
In the midst of the storm.

I spent my life
Providing flame
To try to help
Whoever came.

But foolishly,
I spent so much time giving
That I never poured into
The life I was living.

One day I awoke
And was swallowed in cold.
The light and warmth inside
Had been sold.

The fire inside me
Was now extinguished
Because in giving away,
No self-care was distinguished.

It was then that I knew
That I had to embark
On a difficult journey
To relight a small spark.

This journey was harder
Than any that I knew.
But I believe that
You can do it too.

The physical journey
And the one in my head
Is so exhausting and painful
My heart felt like lead.

It's hard to believe
That I deserve to survive.
But not only that,
We deserve to thrive.

Don't forget that you need
To practice self-care.
Then one day you'll find
That your fire is still there.

Printed in the United States
By Bookmasters